400 Fortn

and Tricks

The Ultimate Battle

Royale Strategy

Guide Book for Kids

and Teens

written permission from the publisher. All rights reserved.

without permission or backing by the trademark owner. All trademarks and brands within this book are for clarifying purposes only and are owned by the owners themselves, not affiliated with this document.

1.   Aim for the head! Headshots do a lot more damage than regular shots and could be the difference between you getting the eliminate and them eliminating you.

2.   Practice shooting in the training area to improve your accuracy + building and/or get familiar with the controls.

3.   Gather materials from the moment you land right after you get a gun. Aim to have at least 100 materials before leaving your house.

4.   Break furniture in the house to
        gather materials quickly.

5.   Keep 70% of your focus on
        building and 30% on shooting
        when you're in a fight.

6.   Use wood in fights since it builds
        the fastest and has the highest
        amount of initial health.

7.   Use brick and metal when building
        a more long term base since they
        have more health when fully built.

8.   Farm fences and trees to get a lot of wood.

9.   Prioritize shields before health since health items are more common and you're going to lose shields before health.

10.   Have at least one close range weapon and one long range weapon. For example, a sniper and SMG.

11.   Practice building either in Playground mode or in a corner of the map when you land so you're comfortable building in a fight.

12. Understand the objective of the game which is to be the last one surviving.

13. Being the last one surviving doesn't mean you should hide because then you will never get better.

14. Be aggressive and try to get into fights as much as possible once you're comfortable with building.

15. Play smart. Aggressive does not mean blindly running into fights. Assess the situation.

16. Invest in a good headset so that you can hear sounds that you otherwise wouldn't hear. Hearing footsteps is just as important as seeing your enemies.

17. Upgrade your weapon's whenever possible either through chests or whenever you eliminate an enemy.

18. Learn the map. Know all the popular spots where people land.

19. Be wary of where people land when you jump off the Battle Bus.

Know how many people are in the area you are landing in.

20.   Pick your fights carefully later in the game. If you don't have enough material for example, then don't engage someone that is posted up in a tower that they've built.

21.   Use the replay system to study your gameplay and analyze your mistakes.

22.   Watch professional players and streamers. Learn from their decision making and movements.

23. Don't get frustrated. It takes time to learn.

24. Practice is key. The more you play, the better you will get as long as you learn from your mistakes.

25. Drop in as many different locations as possible and see what you like the most.

26. Drop in medium to highly populated areas once you learn how to build to engage in early game fights.

27.   Boogie bombs last for 5 seconds
       but any sort of damage will end
       the effect early.

28.   You can double stack campfires
       to double your healing.

29.   You can only place traps on your
       own structures or neutral ones,
       not enemies'.

30.   Hitting the circle with your pickaxe
       when breaking something will do
       double the damage and allow you
       to farm or break the object twice
       as fast.

31.   Aiming your gun towards a tree will let you see its HP which can let you know if enemies have been in the area.

32.   Get on top of a house early game to scope out the area.

33.   Always watch your back so that enemies don't sneak up on you.

34.   Never stand still or you will probably get sniped.

35.   Move as much as possible in a close range gunfight so that you are harder to hit.

36.   Look out for llama spawns. There are a total of 3 in every game.

37.   Spam build whenever you get shot at.

38.   Your first instinct should always be to build when you see an enemy, even if it's as simple as a staircase.

39.   Always think build first, shoot second.

40.   Building two stairs side by side with two walls reinforcing them is a great standard build to learn.

41.   If you need to get higher then you
        can simply repeat the two stairs
        and walls.

42.   If you have the chance of being
        shot from multiple angles, use the
        1x1 structure.

43.   The 1x1 is 4 walls and a staircase
        in the middle.

44.   Port a Fort can be helpful when
        you are getting outbuilt.

45. Throw the Port a Fort underneath your opponents to building to destroy their structure.

46. Block entry to your Port a Fort by placing a floor above the entrance.

47. Rocks are a great source of brick.

48. Mining metal is not worth it. You will only really use it during the end game.

49. A great way of farming materials is by eliminating enemy players

and letting them do the work for you.

50.   Big rocks give less brick than the medium sized rocks.

51.   Leave traps in houses that you loot to get easy eliminations.

52.   Place traps on the ceiling since those are much harder to detect.

53.   Learn how to edit rather than breaking structures.

54. Play with a full squad if possible. More often than not, random players don't even stick with you which puts you at a disadvantage against other full squads.

55. Communicate with your teammates at all times including your position and where you want to move.

56. Move as a group rather than independently.

57. Use the compass to point out enemies or directions. Specifically, try to use the

numbers so that you're as accurate as possible.

58.   When sieging enemy players that are camping, try to spot weak points in their base that can make it collapse.

59.   If you have a grenade launcher, you can break enemy bases very fast.

60.   If you have a rocket launcher, shoot at the base of their tower rather than at the top since they won't be able to rebuild the bottom.

61.　　　If you are going to play with random players in squads, have a mic so you can communicate with them.

62.　　　Try to learn as much as possible from these random players if they are experienced. See how they play and how they move around the map.

63.　　　If there are multiple players rushing you and you see them coming from a distance, run away and try to get a better vantage point unless you are confident you can eliminate them.

64.   When facing multiple enemies, you have to be able to shoot a lot more in between building or else they will be able to destroy your buildings faster than you can build.

65.   In general, you always want to be shooting at your enemy whenever you see an opening but still keep a focus on building.

66.   Before going online, try to get a full squad going by contacting your friends that may not be online.

67.   You can use tires to get onto higher floors of building.

68.   Using ramps and floors, you can climb buildings easily.

69.   Land in as many spots as possible so that you have a feel for the map. This is important in case the circle closes in on an unfamiliar area.

70.   However, focus on mastering 2 or 3 spots so that you know where all the chests and best vantage points are.

71.   Don't build around trees. They get in the way and restrict mobility.

72.   If you start building around a tree and realize later, take the 2 seconds to chop it down.

73.   Bandages only heal till 75 health.

74.   Mushrooms heal 5 shield. Pay attention to them on the ground.

75.   Apples heal 5 health. Pay attention to them on the ground. They can refill your health

completely after you've used bandages.

76.   Mini potions only give you your first 50 shield. They don't work after that.

77.   For the remaining 50, you need either a large potion, chug jug, mushrooms, or a slurp juice.

78.   Chug jugs completely heal your health and shields.

79.   However, use them only if you know you are safe because they take 15 seconds to consume.

80.   Slurp juice slowly regenerates 25 health and 25 shield.

81.   Slurp juice is great to use after using bandages and if you are low on shield.

82.   Be careful after eliminating an enemy. More may be approaching.

83.   After eliminating an enemy, they have seen the loot from the body, therefore be cautious because there may be someone tracking you.

84.	The storm progressively does more damage as the game goes on.

85.	The storm moves fast in the beginning of the game but then slows down as the game progresses.

86.	The circle closes in faster in some parts compared to others.

87.	If it has less area to cover, then it will move slower since the time till it closes is constant.

88.   You can afford to take some damage early from the storm therefore do not panic if you are caught in it.

89.   Use rifts to escape from the storm if you get caught.

90.   Use rifts to escape from enemies if you are disadvantaged.

91.   After early game, never fight enemies without having at least 300 material.

92. When camping in a base, edit to create windows so you have another point to shoot from.

93. Peek only enough from behind a wall and staircase so that you can see your enemy otherwise you may get sniped.

94. Take advantage of the 3rd person camera to peek around corners.

95. Since your character is slightly to the left off center, try to peek to the right since you have a greater field of vision.

96.   Be careful doing a dance or other emote after getting an elimination, you may get shot at from nearby enemies.

97.   Pay attention to the sound of gunshots to locate enemies.

98.   Campfires still heal you even if you build a ramp over top of them.

99.   My personal favorite streamer to learn from is SypherPK since he has educational commentaries.

100.   Optimize your keybindings on PC.

101.   Look up pro player's keybindings to emulate if you don't have a preference for your own.

102.   Invest in a gaming mouse or keyboard for more macros that can make some of the controls easier.

103.   For console, be sure to use builder pro since it will allow you to build seamlessly.

104.   Try switching your right stick click and x buttons so that clicking the right stick allows you to jump.

That will allow you to maintain your aim while jumping in fights.

105.   You can also try playing claw if you don't want to switch your button layout.

106.   If an enemy is building a base to camp in, build up to them with the same material so it masks your ambush.

107.   Try to line up easy headshots on enemies that haven't see you yet.

108.   Lead your shots slightly to get
        better accuracy.

109.   With snipers, you may have to
        lead quite a bit depending on how
        far you are from the enemy and
        how they are moving.

110.   Crouch when you shoot to get
        better accuracy.

111.   Only crouch in mid to long range
        shooting. Close range, maximize
        mobility.

112.   If someone is building up to you, block them with a floor.

113.   Use editing to eliminate enemies that think they are safe.

114.   Add random players that you enjoy playing with so you can play with them again.

115.   Fortnite has bullet drop therefore this needs to be taken into account.

116.   At medium to long range, tap fire with your rifles to maximize accuracy.

117. Only fully hold down the trigger at close range.

118. Abandon your base if you are getting shot at from multiple places.

119. Listen to if someone is shooting the base of your tower. Sometimes it can be difficult to hear.

120. Always be looking around when camping. It is easy for enemies to sneak up.

121. Try not to build more than 3 stories since you will take fall damage when higher than that.

122. Try to build on high elevations.

123. Examples of high elevations are houses, buildings, and hills.

124. Height advantage is the most important advantage you can have on another player.

125. Ramp rushing is a great offensive tactic.

126.   Building two walls in a L shape with a staircase in the middle then repeating the process is a great way to gain vertical distance.

127.   If someone starts ramp rushing towards you, start ramping right away as well.

128.   If you get on top of them, you can edit the ramp and drop on them and eliminate them.

129.   If they get a ramp over you, quickly build to the side and start building vertically again.

130.   If you are streaming, remember to add a delay so you don't get stream sniped.

131.   When you launch into the air with a jump pad, you take no fall damage.

132.   Use jump pads on ramps or walls to cover distance quickly.

133.   Launch pads and rifts, however, are the best ways to navigate the map quickly since you deploy a parachute.

134.   Build high before using a launch
       pad otherwise you won't go very
       far.

135.   You can use launch pads to get
       out of fights that you are at a
       disadvantage.

136.   When running in a squad, be sure
       there is someone who is carrying
       health items and someone who is
       carrying shields.

137.   Have a mix of weapons in your
       squad such as grenade launchers
       and snipers.

138.   However, make sure everyone
        has basic essential weapons such
        as an AR and SMG or shotgun.

139.   If you accidentally split off from
        your squad and you get
        ambushed, let your squad know
        but in the meantime, box yourself
        in with 4 walls and a floor.

140.   You can place a pyramid on top of
        the roof for an extra layer.

141.   You can put a ramp inside your
        box for an extra layer.

142. No need to jump when you place a jump pad underneath you. It will activate right away.

143. If someone uses a rocket launcher close range, build walls in front of you. More often than not, they will eliminate themselves.

144. Ghost peek by aiming then crouching up and down from behind a wall. In between, take shots and you are very hard to hit.

145. Shoot through cracks of buildings to eliminate unsuspecting enemies.

146. Take your shots carefully in squads. Just because you see someone, doesn't mean you should shoot. Coordinate with your team.

147. Take down llamas by using your pickaxe instead. This makes it faster and makes you harder to hit while looting.

148. When looting, place walls around you so you don't get shot.

149. Pay attention to crates in the sky. They always contain at least one legendary.

150. Use the minigun to eliminate opponent bases quickly rather than an assault rifle.

151. However, be careful since you are not very mobile with a minigun.

152. Don't completely destroy large trees when farming since it is very noticeable when you do.

153. C4s are great for taking down bases and any kind of structure but you have to get close enough.

154. When landing at the beginning of the game, dive over water to deploy your parachute as late as possible. This allows you to land faster.

155. Valleys and rivers are also great for landing faster.

156. Deploy your parachute early if you are trying to reach a far point on the map.

157.   Pay attention to the storm at all times so it doesn't creep up on you.

158.   Try to predict where the next circle is going to be and move towards it early so you don't get caught in the storm.

159.   Most enemies tend to be concentrated at the edge of the circles.

160.   Take note of the path of the battle bus. Along that line is where you will find most of your enemies.

161. Look towards the storm after you are safe for enemies that are coming out of it. These are easy kills.

162. Shopping carts are great for mobility even if you ride it alone.

163. Be careful using the golf carts since they are quite loud and easy to hear.

164. Always build walls around you or take cover when healing or shielding up.

165.   Use movement to help with aiming instead of solely your mouse or right stick.

166.   Hop rocks are great for covering distances.

167.   Be careful using them in fights since they are hard to build with.

168.   When someone lands on the roof of a house with you, prioritize finding a gun before going for a chest.

169.   If they find a gun before you, try to break some furniture quickly and

build a wall then go look for a gun quickly.

170.   Look for sky bases later on towards the game and shoot it down for an easy kill.

171.   Always try to peek and shoot rather than fully exposing yourself.

172.   If you fall more than 3 stories try to catch yourself with either a floor or ramp piece.

173.   See if you like burst weapons more or fully automatic. Mostly it's personal preference.

174. However, fully autos are able to shoot down structures much faster than bursts.

175. There is a secret basement in the light blue house in Salty Springs which has lots of loot.

176. You don't take fall damage when you take a hop rock.

177. Default skin players are not always noobs.

178. Players with skins are not always good players.

179. Assume all your enemies are good players so you don't get caught off guard.

180. Don't get frustrated. Just hop into another game and keep improving.

181. If you do get frustrated, take a break and come back later.

182. Playing frustrated will only make you play worse and hate the game.

183.   Keep a balance in your life
       between Fortnite and other
       activities.

184.   If you are going through a period
       of not playing well, try taking a
       couple days off and coming back
       later. Often times, you will play
       much better.

185.   If you are frustrated before even
       playing, do not play Fortnite
       because it will probably get worse.

186.   Jump in water rather than running
       through it if you are out of
       material.

187. If you have enough material, build a ramp then floors to cross.

188. Avoid the water if possible because you are very vulnerable in it.

189. Do not go into the middle of loot lake since you are very exposed.

190. Try to limit spots where enemies can shoot you. For example, have your back towards the storm where you know no one is going to come from.

191. Hold down the trigger before throwing grenades to see where it is going to go.

192. Avoid using the bush consumable since it is distracting and impedes your aim.

193. If you want to troll and mess around, use the bush.

194. Never camp in bushes (not the consumable) because you will never improve.

195. Shotguns can be quite inconsistent. SMGs are typically much better.

196. Crouch around to mask the sound of your footsteps.

197. Jumping on tires negates fall damage.

198. Use challenges to get through battle pass tiers quickly.

199. Consider purchasing the battle pass, if you buy it once and complete all the challenges for V Bucks, you can theoretically

unlock all future battle passes for free.

200.   Do not panic when you see enemies. Instead, get excited and see them as an elimination.

201.   When building, don't go too crazy and forget to shoot. You want to maintain a balance.

202.   When you make it to endgame, look for the high ground and build high enough that you can see everything.

203. Always run through the perimeter of towns and areas to minimize the sides you can get shot from.

204. Always be gathering resources while running around.

205. In the endgame, you should ideally have other 1000 resources.

206. The final players left during the endgame will likely know how to build well so be ready.

207. Try to look for campers in towers and snipe them.

208. The bolt action sniper is much better if you are good at sniping since it is a guaranteed kill if you get a headshot.

209. Always be looking for chests and trying to upgrade your items.

210. Think of eliminating enemies as a faster way of looting. Let them do the boring looting for you.

211. Med kits are less rare than bandages so try to use the bandages then find apples if possible.

212.   Mini potions are the most valuable consumables since they can be used in between fights.

213.   If you get hit from far away and lose shields, cover yourself and heal up before the enemy closes in.

214.   If you get damaged in the middle of a fight, build up or box yourself in and heal.

215.   If you do damage to an enemy from far away, close in on them quick before they have time to heal.

216. If you damage an enemy in a fight, keep up the pressure so they don't get a chance to heal.

217. Complete the daily challenges every day.

218. Coordinate with your friends to complete challenges.

219. Jump around while moving in an area. It will make you harder to hit for enemies that may be trying to land a shot.

220. Move unpredictably in open areas so you don't get sniped easily.

221.   If someone tries sniping you from far away and they miss, don't peek out your head from cover until you are certain you know their position.

222.   Don't loot immediately after eliminating an enemy. Try to see if other enemies close in.

223.   Bait other enemies to pick up your previous enemy's loot for an easy kill.

224.   When playing in squads, if you down an enemy, tell your team to rush the enemy because at least

one of the enemies will be trying to revive the downed teammate.

225.   4 against 2 are pretty good odds in your favor.

226.   Run over loot when you take down an enemy to pick up all the essential ammo and materials.

227.   Running over the loot also helps clear the clutter and makes it easier to loot the rest.

228.   Share ammo with your teammates if they are low.

229.   Ask for ammo if you are low.

230.   If you are not able to stay calm in fights, keep practicing building. Eventually, you will develop the confidence and won't panic anymore.

231.   The weapon rarity is grey to green to blue to purple to orange.

232.   One or two tiers of rarity won't make a world of difference so if you missed something, don't worry too much about it.

233.   Rarer weapons have better reload
        times, more damage, and greater
        fire rate.

234.   Rarer snipers in particular will also
        have faster scope times.

235.   Assault rifles are the most
        versatile weapons and should
        always be in your layout.

236.   Keep your close range weapon in
        the slot next to your long range
        weapon so you can easily switch
        if need be.

237.   Don't camp early game. People can easily creep up on you.

238.   Camping early game also means you will have less resources and less ammo.

239.   Keep an eye out for ammo boxes when looting.

240.   Building not only gives color but gives you mobility too.

241.   Build wide when making a base so that it is harder to take down.

242.   Share resources with teammates if they are low.

243.   Ask for resources from teammates if you are low or if they are not as good at building.

244.   Make sure to trade weapons so that everyone has the weapons they are best with.

245.   In squads, if an enemy player is eliminated immediately then the rest of his team is not alive. He was the last man.

246.   If you catch an enemy player alone and down him but not eliminate him, then keep him alive and see if his team shows up to try to revive him.

247.   Don't just listen for sounds, try to focus on what direction they are coming from.

248.   Optimize your sensitivity settings to what you are comfortable with.

249.   Higher sensitivity does not mean better. Generally, with high sensitivity you won't have as good aim.

250.   You can still build fast with a low
        sensitivity.

251.   Don't keep it too low either. Try to
        find a balance.

252.   Be patient with your progress.
        Rome wasn't built in a day and
        you won't magically transform into
        Ninja after a day either.

253.   It's not enough just reading these
        tips, you have to implement them.

254.   If someone lands on the roof of a
        house with you at the beginning of
        the game, you may want to go

through the main entrance or through a different door.

255.   Try to use every possible item at your disposable.

256.   Try to outsmart your opponent rather than always relying on good aim especially in situations.

257.   Building can be used inside a house not just outside which can get you a significant advantage over your opponent.

258.   Build a wall in front of your opponent and wait till he starts

pickaxing then quickly edit and take him out.

259.   Learn how to reset your edit in case you make a mistake or need to close an opening.

260.   Always try to think of what advantage you can gain over your opponent.

261.   Try to make it as easy as possible for yourself to eliminate your opponent.

262.   Don't break the floor beneath the chest or the chest will disappear.

263.   Be careful when you hear a chest and you are breaking floors to get to it. You may accidentally destroy it.

264.   Be cautious when exiting a house because someone may be waiting for you to come out.

265.   When fighting an opponent, decide if its best to match their building or simply destroy their structure.

266.   Most often, building will be the way to go but keep the other option in mind.

267.   Close the door behind you when you enter buildings so that it looks like you haven't been there.

268.   When you leave a trap in a house that you've looted, be sure to close the door on the way out so that the enemy is less cautious when entering.

269.   Pressing the jump button before touching the tires will make you jump higher.

270.   All skins are cosmetic only, meaning they do not improve

stats or any game mechanics in any way.

271. Don't spend too much money on Fortnite or you may find yourself in trouble from either your parents or a spouse.

272. The battle pass unlocks challenges which adds a new dimension of fun to the game.

273. Try out the limited time game modes. They are a great variation to the standard battle royale gamemode.

274. Getting a victory royale will unlock some special gear such as a seasonal victory umbrella as a glider.

275. Try to predict where people may be. Think about where would you go next to predict their movement.

276. Know when to disengage from a fight. If you are at a disadvantage, try to disengage by using rift grenades or launch pads.

277. Use supply drop crates as bait to secure easy eliminations.

278. There is a slight moment of invincibility when you down an enemy in squads. Don't keep firing blindly at the downed enemy to secure a kill, try to eliminate the other ones that are alive if they are shooting at you.

279. Don't hog all the good items for yourself. Share loot with your team.

280. Once you get better at building, practice building with using as few resources as possible. This will make you more efficient and you

won't have to farm as much for material.

281. Use your potions whenever possible. Don't think about saving them for a better time when you can get more shield out of them. You may not get the chance.

282. If you have extra healing items, use them even if it's to heal 5 health. You will survive some fights with just 5 health.

283. Experiment with different building patterns and see what works the best for you.

284. When someone is hiding in a house, building floors around the house and try to shoot them through the windows.

285. Don't chase enemies that run into houses or other enclosures. This is called turtling and they will most likely eliminate you if you chase.

286. Fish them out instead by using grenades or other explosives.

287. Another way to take them out is to simply build a small base outside of the house and wait for them to come out.

288.   Keep a good balance between surviving and engaging in fights once you have enough experience.

289.   If your structure doesn't have a connection to the ground, it will collapse.

290.   Re-order your items so that it is convenient for you.

291.   Careful with ramp rushing. You have to shoot them before they shoot your ramps down.

292.   Ramp rushing without walls is risky because you may not be able to shoot them before they shoot down your ramps. Walls provide reinforcement.

293.   Enable turbo building in settings.

294.   Never try to kill someone with a pickaxe unless you have no other option at all.

295.   Pickaxe fights will leave you with little health even if you do win them.

296. All the secret challenge locations can be found using Google instead of trying to decipher the treasure maps.

297. If someone else wants to play on your account, encourage them to do the challenges for you.

298. Play with friends whenever possible. Fortnite is much more fun playing with others than alone.

299. Try Save the World for another angle of Fortnite.

300.   Don't farm cars for metal. They make a lot of noise because the car alarms go off.

301.   Always read the patch notes for the latest updates to the game.

302.   Once you get better at building, try to keep your fights at shorter ranges since building plays a greater role in outplaying your opponent.

303.   Once you have mastered building, try to master editing.

304. Always move around when farming materials. Don't stay in one spot and pickaxe away or you will be an easy target.

305. If you don't have money to invest in a headset, use the earphones that come with your phone. They are still much better than your TV speakers.

306. Sit close enough to your screen that you can clearly see everything.

307.   Adjust your brightness or other settings that will help you clearly see.

308.   Always sit square to your screen and not at an angle.

309.   This may not sound like much but always stay hydrated.

310.   Sleep is very important. You will play a lot worse if you are tired or fatigued.

311.   Try to exercise as much as possible. It improves your energy

levels and overall health which will indirectly make you better at Fortnite.

312. If you haven't showered yet that day and are getting frustrated, take a shower and come back. You will notice you feel a lot more refreshed and re-energized.

313. Try playing on monitors rather than big TV's. You won't have to dart your eyes nearly as much and will be able to see everything a lot more easily.

314.   Try out gaming accessories to see
        if they help your game. Some
        people swear by accessories such
        as Kontrol Freeks for console in
        order to aim for example.

315.   Building is intimidating for other
        players. Many players will
        immediately panic when they see
        a good player.

316.   Do not move around when
        shooting if you have free shots on
        someone. It will only make you
        less accurate.

317. When you land on the roof with someone and you want to risk going for the chest, let them open it and take the items. Don't open it yourself.

318. Use rocket riding to survive the Storm. One person will have to stay back however.

319. Panicking is counterproductive.

320. You can permanently mark a supply drop by shooting it.

321.   You can make supply drops come
down faster by shooting them
down.

322.   Start off in open areas such as
Anarchy Acres to practice building
and fighting.

323.   Turtling is much harder in open
areas.

324.   If you hear someone shooting a
grenade launcher at you, be
mobile. Don't stand still.

325. If you want to troll some people, you can hide in trees and shoot unsuspecting enemies.

326. If you ride the Battle Bus till the end and fall down, you can get 1 or 2 AFK eliminations.

327. Whenever you see structures, it is a good sign that someone is close by.

328. When you see 2 people fighting each other, you can usually take them both out.

329. When two people are build battling and they are high enough, shoot down their structure and eliminate them both.

330. Experiment with different loadouts to see what you like best.

331. Using the quick switch technique. Shoot initially with a burst weapon then immediately switch to a fully automatic to finish them off.

332. Burst weapons include shotguns and sniper rifles.

333.　Constantly be moving at the end game towards the center of the circle.

334.　Wooden pallets are a great source of wood when there are no trees.

335.　Avoid pistols.

336.　You can no longer edit to peek.

337.　Pick up as many items as possible at the beginning of the game.

338.   Slide down hills backwards while walking into it to eliminate fall damage.

339.   Down your allies when they are below 30 health and revive them. They will be up to 30 health.

340.   Build pyramids on top of your floors whenever possible to reinforce it.

341.   Establish loot routes for your favorite areas.

342. Play with your favorite guns. Don't use guns just because they are overpowered if you don't like them.

343. Keep your inventory loadout the same every game.

344. Be able to switch weapons without looking at them.

345. Work on your awareness and always know where other players are.

346. When ramping up to someone, build ramps above you when

possible in order to protect yourself from that angle.

347.   Use bait such as unopened chests in a house to lure enemies into traps.

348.   Stop blaming other factors for your deaths.

349.   Always think what you could have done better.

350.   Record your gameplay and analyze it regularly.

351.   Jumping on top of golf carts lets you jump higher.

352.   While getting the high jump from golf carts, hold down walls to build a 3 story base. Remember to build a floor or ramp at the end so you don't fall back down.

353.   Build floors underneath your ramps to reinforce your structure.

354.   Be cautious when going into houses. Other players may have laid traps.

355. Always check the ceilings whenever entering rooms or houses.

356. Make sure to be outside of the range of the Boogie Bomb or you will be dancing as well.

357. Use auto run to organize your inventory while running.

358. Don't be cheap with your material. Spam it if need be.

359. Reload your shotguns while jumping so you can reload while moving.

360.   The pyramid structure can be
        edited into a ramp.

361.   Use two C4s instead of one when
        someone is turtled up. The
        second one will actually do
        damage to them. This applies to
        all explosives.

362.   You can rotate your structures.

363.   Complete the challenges to level
        up your Battle Pass fast.

364.   Switch into the basket of the
        shopping cart after getting speed
        to shoot from it when solo.

365.   Teamwork makes the dream work.

366.   The minigun and rocket launcher can give the shopping cart massive speed boosts.

367.   If you land correctly, shopping carts negate fall damage.

368.   Using the pyramid can make it much easier to get into windows in places like Tilted Towers.

369.   If you and a downed friend are stuck in the Storm, use the launch

pad to move them through it quickly.

370.   Put a pyramid over a downed ally to protect them.

371.   Instead of boxing yourself with 4 walls and a floor, use one pyramid instead.

372.   Use floors and pyramids if you are building a skybase.

373.   A skybase is made by building very high from the edge of the

map then making your way
towards the center.

374.   Generally you are so high up that
people won't notice you.

375.   The shopping cart boost
technique also works in water.

376.   Certain skins will make you much
more noticeable to other enemies.

377.   Using the default skin may make
people underestimate you, giving
you the advantage.

378. Using a skin, however, may give you an disadvantage because people may overestimate you.

379. Double pump shotgunning no longer works.

380. Place traps inside your tower in case someone glides in from above.

381. Have an escape plan in a fight in case it gets too heated.

382. If someone is pushing towards you aggressively, placing a trap down may deter them.

383.   You can box someone in with 4
        walls and place a trap inside to
        eliminate them.

384.   Use jump pads to build vertically
        very fast.

385.   Fortnite is cross platform meaning
        you can play with your friends
        even if they are on different
        systems.

386.   To improve your aim, look up
        aiming drills that you can practice.

387.   Fortnite has bloom meaning that your shots will go somewhere between your crosshairs.

388.   Make sure aim assist is turned on if you are playing on console.

389.   PC does not have aim assist.

390.   Aim assist is made for consoles to compensate for not having a mouse since joysticks are less accurate.

391.   Sometimes it can be better not to move while fighting an enemy especially at medium range and

when you are behind cover. This will increase your accuracy.

392.   If you stand still and aim down with an AR or SMG, you will get 100% accuracy for your first shot.

393.   Your 100% accuracy shots do less damage than normal shots.

394.   You can use impulse grenades to cover distances faster.

395.   You can also accidentally eliminate yourself with impulse

nades by throwing yourself off a
cliff so be careful.

396.   An easy way to kill an enemy
when you both are build battling is
by throwing an impulse nade at
him to make him fall to his death.

397.   Use launch pads and rifts to
sneak up on campers from above.

398.   Look into getting an elite controller
such as a Scuf .

399.   Scufs have paddles on the back
so you can jump around or assign
other buttons to them without

taking your hands off the
joysticks.

400.   There is no friendly fire in Fortnite.

401.   Bonus tip! Keep practicing but
don't forget that at the end of the
day Fortnite is a game and you
are meant to have fun with it!

Made in the USA
Lexington, KY
29 November 2018